SUMMARY

OF

ENLIGHTENMENT NOW:

THE CASE FOR REASON, SCIENCE, HUMANISM, AND PROGRESS

From an Idea of
Steven Pinker

Authored with love by:

better.me

Knowledge for people who crave development

Legal & Disclaimer

The information contained in this book is not designed to replace or take the place of any form of medical or professional advice. The information in this book has been provided for educational purposes only

The information contained in this book has been compiled from sources deemed reliable, and it is accurate to the best of the Author's knowledge; however, the Author cannot guarantee its accuracy and validity and cannot be held liable for any error or omissions. Changes are periodically made to this book. You must consult your doctor for professional medical advice before using any of the suggested remedies, techniques, or information in this book. Images used in this book are not the same as of that of the actual book. This is a separate and different entity from that of the original text titled *Enlightenment Now* by Steven Pinker.

Upon using the information contained in this book, you agree to hold, harmless, the Author from and against any damages, costs, and expenses, including any legal fees potentially resulting from the application of any of the information provided in this guide. This disclaimer applies to any damages or injury caused by the use and application, whether directly or indirectly, of any advice or information presented, whether for breach of contract, tort, negligence, personal injury, criminal intent, or under any other cause of action. You agree to accept all risks of using the information presented in this book.

This is a summary of *Enlightenment Now* by Steven Pinker composed to help you understand modern culture and science better, and adopt an optimistic view of the world.

Most people also buy the original book through this <u>link</u>.

Contents

THE BOOK AT GLANCE

This book has a straightforward aim, visible in its title. It discusses enlightenment in the present world and defends its ideals. The word "enlightenment" in this book should not be understood to mean supernatural wisdom that can resolve all human questions, problems, crises, and doubts. Instead, this book defends the ideals of the 18th century cultural climate known as the Enlightenment. The main principles of the 18th century Enlightenment were the idea of progress, freedom from all forms of superstition (including religious), belief in human reason and science as the only way of achieving progress, and the idea of toleration.

About the Author

Steven Pinker (born in 1954) is a US-Canadian linguist, psychologist, and an author on popular science. He teaches Psychology at Harvard University and specializes in visual cognition and psycholinguistics.

Pinker was born in Montreal, Quebec, where he grew up. He obtained his Bachelor of Arts degree at McGill University in 1973. He completed his Ph.D. at Harvard University in experimental psychology, after which he taught at Harvard and Stanford Universities.

Pinker's research fields include evolutionary and experimental psychology, cognitive sciences, visual cognition, and psycholinguistics. For his contributions in science, he has received many awards and distinctions such as Boyd McCandless Award from the American Psychological Association, Troland Research Award from the National Academy of Sciences, George Miller Prize from the Cognitive Neuroscience Society, etc. Among his most recent and notable publications are the following:

- *The Blank Slate: The Modern Denial of Human Nature* (2002)

- *The Stuff of Thought: Language as a Window into Human Nature* (2007)

- *Language, Cognition, and Human Nature: Selected Articles* (2013)

- *The Sense of Style: The Thinking Person's Guide to Writing in the 21st Century* (2014)

- *Enlightenment Now: The Case for Reason, Science, Humanism, and Progress* (2018)

INTRODUCTION

I want to thank you and congratulate you for downloading the book *Enlightenment Now: The Case for Reason, Science, Humanism, and Progress.*

This book will provide you with the modern restatement of the Enlightenment principles, as interpreted by Steven Pinker. The book will help you gain a better understanding of our world as well as the aims and principles of modern science. It provides arguments for the view that human reason is the ultimate bastion of human progress and happiness.

CHAPTERS OVERVIEW

*E*nlightenment *Now* contains the following parts and chapters:

Part I: Enlightenment

Chapter 1 – Dare to Understand! – In this chapter, the author outlines and discusses the basic ideals of the 18th century Enlightenment, such as reason, science, progress, and humanity. They established the foundation of the contemporary world.

Chapter 2 – Entro, Evo, Info – In this chapter, Steven Pinker discusses the key contemporary ideals that are closely related to the idea of progress: entropy, evolution, and information.

Chapter 3 – Counter-Enlightenments – In this chapter, Steven Pinker has outlined some of the most common counter-Enlightenment theories

Part II: Progress

Chapter 4 – Progressophobia – In this chapter, Steven Pinker reflected on the reasons of what he termed "progressophobia," or a consistent academic and non-academic bias towards the idea of progress

Chapter 5 – Life – In this chapter, Steven Pinker brought out facts that speak in favor of our life expectancy

Chapter 6 – Health – In this chapter, Steven Pinker discussed scientific advancements throughout history, which greatly reduced the amount of lives lost to numerous diseases

Chapter 7 – Sustenance – In this chapter, Steven Pinker discussed some of the major advancements in overcoming famine and increasing food production on a global scale

Chapter 8 – Wealth – In this chapter, Steven Pinker reflected on advancements in global economy and accumulation of wealth

Chapter 9 – Inequality – In this chapter, Steven Pinker provided an in-depth analysis on inequality, which is often emphasized by critics as the woe of modern society

Chapter 10 – The Environment – In this chapter, Steven Pinker discussed common environmental issues and pointed to numerous advances in safeguarding the environment

Chapter 11 – Peace – In this chapter, Steven Pinker discussed the notion of war and how it declined after World War II

Chapter 12 – Safety – In this chapter, Steven Pinker provided a detailed analysis of improved safety on a global scale

Chapter 13 – Terrorism – In this chapter, Steven Pinker discussed the popular topic of terrorism and indicated that the growing fear of terrorist attacks is totally unfounded

Chapter 14 – Democracy – In this chapter, Steven Pinker discussed the concept of *democracy* and how closely it is related to the idea of progress

Chapter 15 – Equal Rights – In this chapter, Steven Pinker analyzed the subject of equal rights and provided statistical analyses that show various advancements in acknowledging civil and human rights

Chapter 16 – Knowledge – In this chapter, Steven Pinker emphasized the concepts of knowledge and education for human progress

Chapter 17 – Quality of Life – In this chapter, Steven Pinker discussed how quality of life today is incomparably better to those of previous eras

Chapter 18 – Happiness – In this chapter, Steven Pinker analyzed the concept of happiness. He concluded that happiness does not depend solely on wealth and being healthy

Chapter 19 – Existentialism – In this chapter, Steven Pinker discussed some of the most popular existential threats

Chapter 20 – The Future of Progress – In this chapter, Steven Pinker outlined both negative and positive sides of the progress. He maintains that it is humanity's imperative to strive for the progress

Part III: Reason, Science, and Humanism

Chapter 21 – Reason – In this chapter, Steven Pinker discusses the concept of reason and its role in modern Enlightenment

Chapter 22 – Science – In this chapter, Steven Pinker critically analyzed positive aspects and criticism of science

Chapter 23 – Humanism – In this chapter, Steven Pinker discussed the concept of humanity as one of the principle Enlightenment's ideals

This book will provide you with the modern restatement of the Enlightenment principles, as interpreted by Steven Pinker. The book will help you gain a better understanding of our world as well as the aims and principles of modern science. It provides arguments for the view that human reason is the ultimate bastion of human progress and happiness.

BOOK INTRODUCTION

Steven Pinker introduced his book by evoking his memory of an arresting question which he was asked by one of his students. The question came after his explanation of the commonplace among scientists that mental life consists of activity patterns within our brain tissues. A student raised her hand and asked him:

"Why should I live?"

The tone of the question was neither suicidal nor sarcastic. It reflected the student's desire to understand the meaning and purpose of life when traditional religious beliefs of the soul's immortality have been undermined by contemporary science. Pinker's reply was a lengthy one, but its core principle was man's ability to progress by refining his or her reason through learning. He also added that we could enrich ourselves by appreciating beauty and richness of our natural and cultural world, and by perpetuating life. Recognizing that these faculties are not limited to certain individuals, man can sympathize with others and contribute to the general progress of humankind by improving the human condition.

Having recounted this short story, the author presents his aims of defending the Enlightenment ideals of reason, science, humanism, and progress. Pinker recognizes these human traits as instrumental in shaping the contemporary society which today has fewer armed conflicts, continuous medical and technical advancements, and a rich history of human culture available almost to everyone. He is convinced that the ideals of Enlightenment require vigorous defense because people raise doubts in human reason. They can become cynical about the Enlightenment-inspired institutions that facilitate the progress (for instance, liberal democracy and organizations of international corporation). The Enlightenment's ideals have always struggled with "other strands of human nature", such as loyalty to tribe, deference to authority, the blaming of misfortune on evildoers, etc. By quoting other eminent authors, Pinker supports his defense of Enlightenment's ideals:

- "The West is shy of its values – it doesn't speak up for classical liberalism" (Shiraz Maher).

- "If old truths are to retain their hold on men's minds, the must be restated in the language and concepts of successive generations" (Friedrich Hayek).

Finally, Pinker makes it clear that his aim is to "restate the ideals of the Enlightenment in the language and concepts of the 21st century." Far from anachronic, he considers these ideals to be stirring, inspiring, and noble. In brief, they are a reason to live.

In the Introduction of his book, Steven Pinker outlined the main reasons why he has taken up such a large task:

- Enlightenment ideals are worth discussing even today.

- The ideals of reason, science, progress, and humanity are sound and right.

- In our time these ideals should be defended more strongly than ever.

- Enlightenment ideals should not be taken for granted. They are the most responsible for progress in any sphere of human society.

- Enlightenment ideals are the reason to live.

Part I
Enlightenment

Chapter 1

DARE TO UNDERSTAND!

Immanuel Kant established the principles of Enlightenment near the end of the 18th century. In his famous 1784 essay *What is Enlightenment?* he defined it as man's "emergence from his self-incurred immaturity" and from "lazy and cowardly" acceptance of "dogmas and formulas" imposed by political and religious authority. However, Enlightenment was never an official organization or creed, such as, for instance, religion. Yet its principles are widely recognized. David Deutsch, a 21-century physicist restated the defense of Enlightenment's principles in his book *The Beginning of Infinity.* Echoing Kant's famous statement, he claimed that progress is possible in scientific, politic, moral, and all other fields if we dare to understand.

The Enlightenment is usually situated in the 18th century, but its roots can be found in the Scientific

Revolution and the Age of Reason in the 17th century. Most philosophers and men of science proposed a plethora of ideas during the Age of Reason, but four main themes bind these ideas together: reason, science, humanism, and progress.

Reason – Human reason is the bastion of science and all progress. It is the foremost ideal of the Enlightenment. The 17th and 18th century thinkers constantly emphasized that men should "energetically apply the standard of reason to understand" their world. This means they should reject delusions such as faith, dogma, authority, mysticism, visions, divination, etc. Pinker describes that "the application of reason revealed that reports of miracles were dubious, that the authors of holy books were all too human, that natural events unfolded with no regard to human welfare, and that different cultures believed in mutually incompatible deities."

Science – Science refines reason to understand the world. It rejects all superstition and uses methods such as skepticism, fallibilism, open debates, and empirical testing to achieve objective knowledge. It also includes an understanding of ourselves.

Humanism – Philosophers of the 17th and 18th century often spoke of the universal human nature. They "saw an urgent need for a secular foundation for morality, because they were haunted by a historical memory of centuries of religious carnage: the Crusades, the Inquisition, witch hunts, the European wars of religion." Humanism implies acceptance of individual men as opposed to tribes, races, and nations. Individuals, not groups, are sentient beings, i.e., they are able to feel pleasure, pain, and fulfillment. Our human nature equipped us with the feeling of sympathy or the capacity to sympathize with others.

Progress – Enlightenment's ideal of progress was focused toward human institutions, such as governments, laws, schools, markets, etc. Therefore, governments shouldn't be understood as divine institutions, but purely human systems designed to foster the welfare of citizens. As the Enlightenment's most famous document, the Declaration of

Independence, states, "in order to secure the right to life, liberty, and the pursuit of happiness, governments are instituted among people, deriving their just powers from the consent of the government."

Enlighteners' thoughts about reason and progress also included state-related subjects, such as prosperity as well as accumulation and distribution of wealth. Adam Smith realized that economic activity, such as exchange of goods and services, was mutually beneficial cooperation. He concluded that by working for their own well being, individuals also work for the benefit of whole society.

In Chapter 1 of his book, Steven Pinker discusses some of the most fundamental ideals of the Enlightenment and reaches important conclusions:

- German philosopher Immanuel Kant defined Enlightenment as "man's emergence from his self-incurred immaturity."

- The basic ideals of Enlightenment, which laid the foundations of our world, were *reason*, *science*, *progress*, and *humanity*.

- The thinkers of Enlightenment understood that if humanity is to achieve progress, it must reject superstitions such as religious dogmas and faith, mysticism, fanaticism, irrationalism.

- Important American figures of the Enlightenment, such as Adam Smith, George Washington, James Madison, and Alexander Hamilton, designed institutions of the young nation to nurture it.

Chapter 2

ENTRO, EVO, INFO

Rational as they were, Enlightenment thinkers never figured out critical ideas (from our point of view) that would make their progress more certain. The author suggests these ideas are *entropy*, *evolution*, and *information*. They are the keystones to understanding the human condition.

Entropy – The key to understanding this concept is the Second Law of Thermodynamics. It states that in an isolated system (one that is not interacting with its environment), entropy never decreases. In other words, "closed systems inexorably become less structured, less organized, less able to accomplish interesting and useful outcomes, until they slide into an equilibrium of grey, tepid, homogenous monotony and stay there." Entropy has a sustained effect on our everyday lives and our position in the universe. Our life and happiness depend on an orderly arrangement of matter against an infinite number of possibilities. This means that when things change without a human agent controlling the change, they will most likely become worse.

Evolution – This aspect of nature represents an orderliness within living creatures or organisms. They resist entropy by using the energy to maintain their integrity. As opposed to most creationists' claims, organisms are open systems: "they capture energy from the sun, food, or ocean vents to carve out temporary pockets of order in their bodies and nests while they dump heat and waste into the environment, increasing disorder in the world as a whole."

Information – Information could be interpreted as reduction in entropy. Some physicists include it among the basic constituents of the universe, along with matter and energy. A brain not only stores and organizes information from the senses but is also capable of transforming it such that it reflects the laws that govern the world. That enables us to make useful inferences and predictions about the world. In addition, we can thus observe physical systems as teleological, i.e., containing goals and purposes. This "energy channeled by knowledge is the elixir with which we stave off entropy, and advances in energy capture are advances in human destiny."

The concepts of *entro, evo, and info* define the narrative of human progress. Even though there is still much superstition even today (as men are not born learned), they path to progress can be made clear with an understanding of these crucial ideas. Therefore, the author concludes that "for all the flaws in human nature, it contains the seeds of its own improvement, as long as it comes up with norms and institutions that channel parochial interests into universal benefits."

In Chapter 2 of his book, Steven Pinker discussed the key ideas and theses for the contemporary progress of humankind:

- We need to have the awareness of entropy in order to have effective control of the processes in our lives. Without our influence and control, everything that surrounds us will have a negative effect on our lives.

- The Second Law of Thermodynamics states that entropy never decreases in an isolated system. This shows us that humans are the only agents that are responsible for what happens to them.

- The theory of evolution gained impetus during the 19th century. Evolution reveals the complexity of our organism and its ability to resist entropy.

- Information is sometimes wrongly interpreted as being a nuisance in our lives. But if we observe it from a different perspective, we can understand that our brain is able to process any amount of information better than any computer. It allows us to reach important conclusions that will affect our lives positively.

- Entropy, evolution, and information are the building blocks of our present state. We can maintain and improve our society and lives if we understand these crucial ideas and reject prejudice and superstition.

Chapter 3

COUNTER-ENLIGHTENMENTS

The ideals of reason, science, humanism, and progress may sound appealing to anyone. However, since the 18th century, Enlightenment has had its share of opponents. Back then, some of them were famous philosophers and writers, such as Rousseau, Herder, and Schelling. Nowadays, those who usually oppose Enlightenment's ideals are the same ones who support religious faith and nationalism.

A common criticism of the Enlightenment ideals is that they are unsuited for the world in all its diversity. However, these ideals can be considered universal because they are rooted in reason and human nature. Even though they stem from 18th century Europe and the U.S., they have gained resonance in non-Western countries.

Religious faith is among the most common counter-Enlightenment ideals because faith in the existence of supernatural entities clashes with reason. "Belief in an afterlife implies that health and happiness are not such a big deal, because life on earth infinitesimal portion of one's existence."

Aside from religious faith, *nationalism* is another common form of counter-Enlightenment. It situates a particular nation and/or state as superorganism which is above human happiness and prosperity. It's aims are reflected in morbid patriotic slogans, such as "Sweet and right is to die for your country." On the other hand, nationalism should not be confused with cultural pride, civic values, or social responsibility.

More counter-Enlightenment criticism comes from left-wing environmentalists. They are convinced that "resisting entropy and enhancing human flourishing" destroys nature by spoiling water, air, and climate. While this may be true, it would be silly to claim that our technologically advanced society is unable to do anything about it.

Further attempts to refute the Enlightenment ideals come from writers who proclaim consistent decline of modern society. The historian Arthur Herman recounts two centuries of writers "who have sounded the alarm of racial, cultural, political, or ecological degeneration." According to them, the world has been coming to an end for quite some time.

In Chapter 3, Steven Pinker has outlined some of the most common counter-Enlightenment theories:

- With its belief in cosmic deities, religious faith often clashes with the ideals of reason and progress.

- Nationalism is a form of counter-Enlightenment which puts nations and races above anything else.

- Environmentalists claim that progress has brought about the downfall of natural environment and that this cannot be stopped.

- Numerous other counter-Enlightenment principles and theories have come from various writers during the past two centuries. They think that the world is steadily coming to an end.

Part II
Progress

Chapter 4

PROGRESSOPHOBIA

Surprising or even shocking as it may sound, many intellectuals remain blind to or simply reject the idea that progress enhances society. Ordinary people too have become, in most cases, rather pessimistic about the course of future. The reasons for such growing negativity are not hard to find. Every day the news reports about terrorism, war, pollution, inequality, oppression, etc. People tend to base their opinions and beliefs on what they usually see on television. Psychologists Amos Tversky and Daniel Kahneman called this occurrence the "Availability heuristics." Pinker concludes that "availability errors are a common source of folly in human reasoning. [...] Plane crashes always make the news, but car crashes, which kill far more people, almost never do. Not surprisingly, many people have a fear of flying, but almost no one has a fear of driving."

Obviously, journalistic habits will continue to exert adverse effects on general population. But Pinker showed that the reality regarding violence in general is different. In his 2011 book *The Better Angels of our Nature*, Pinker proved that violence and conditions that foster it have declined over the course of history. Yet the decline in violence is not linear, as some may think. "Progress cannot always be monotonic because solutions to problems create new problems."

Pinker's claim that violence has declined over time was met with criticism to which he responded in this chapter of his book:

Criticism: "*To say that violence has gone down is to be naïve, sentimental, idealistic, romantic, starry-eyed, Whiggish, utopian, a Pollyanna, a Pangloss.*"

Answer: "No, to look at data showing that violence has gone down and say 'Violence has gone down' is to describe a fact. To look at data showing that violence has gone down and say 'Violence has gone up' is to be delusional. To ignore data on violence and say 'Violence has gone up' is to be a know-nothing."

Criticism: *"How can you predict that violence will keep going down? Your theory could be refuted by a war breaking out tomorrow."*

Answer: "A statement that some measure of violence has gone down is not a 'theory' but an observation of a fact. And yes, the fact that a measure has changed over time is not the same as a prediction that it will continue to change in that way at all times forever."

Criticism: *"In that case, what good are all those graphs and analyses? Isn't a scientific theory supposed to make testable predictions?"*

Answer: "A scientific theory makes predictions in *experiments* in which the causal influences are controlled. No theory can make a prediction about the world at large, with its seven billion people spreading viral ideas in global networks and interacting with chaotic cycles of weather and resources."

In Chapter 4 of his book, Steven Pinker reflected on the reasons of what he termed "progressophobia," or a consistent academic and non-academic bias towards the idea of progress:

- Many intellectuals and common people fail to see the benefits of progress.

- The general pessimism regarding the progress in today's world can be attributed to the majority of news reports that focus on negative content.

- Psychologists Amos Tversky and Daniel Kahneman coined the term "Availability heuristics" to designate the negative influence of news on most people's judgements.

- In his 2011 book *The Better Angels of our Nature*, Pinker concluded that violence has declined in the course of history, even though it has the tendency to go up and down.

- Steven Pinker refuted criticism on his observation about the decline of violence.

Chapter 5

LIFE

Thᵢs chapter opens up with the discussion and facts of life expectancy. Max Roser's figure displays a global life expectancy starting from the latter 18th century till 2015.

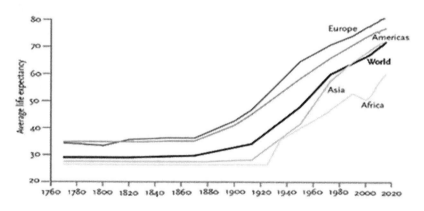

Figure 5-1: Life expectancy, 1771–2015

Sources: Our World in Data, Roser 2016n, based on data from Riley 2005 for the years before 2000 and from the World Health Organization and the World Bank for the subsequent years. Updated with data provided by Max Roser.

The figure 5-1 shows that life expectancy began to rise in the 20th century. The economic historian, Johan Norberg, points out that during the twentieth century, the average person approached death at a significantly slower pace than what was usually thought. Pinker also showed drastically lower mortality rates in children and mothers, with the exception of a few countries.

Figure 5-2: Child mortality, 1751–2013

Sources: *Our World in Data*, Roser 2016a, based on data from the UN Child Mortality estimates, http://www.childmortality.org/, and the *Human Mortality Database*, http://www.mortality.org/.

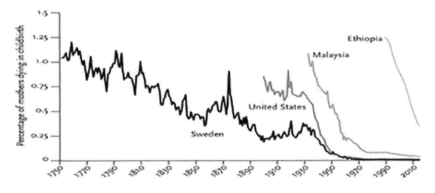

Figure 5-3: Maternal mortality, 1751–2013

The author's argument is that no matter how old we are, we have more years ahead of us than people in past decades and centuries. He also emphasizes the finding of the economist Steven Radelet: "The improvements in health among the global poor in the last few decades are so large and widespread that they rank among the greatest achievements in human history. [...] Yet few people are even aware that it is happening."

Furthermore, the additional years we spend will not be the years of enduring sufferings in old age. Pinker reminds us that "bodies that are better at resisting a mortal blow are also better at resisting the lesser assaults of disease, injury, and wear."

In Chapter 5 of his book, Steven Pinker brought out facts that speak in favor of our life expectancy. He concluded the following:

- Life expectancy was rather low in the past, but it assumed a rising trend from the end of the 18th century.

- During the 20th century, the average person approached death at a significantly slower pace than what was usually thought.

- Child and pregnant mother mortality was consistently reduced from the second half of the 18th century until today.

- Despite pessimistic opinions about life expectancy today, numbers and facts tell a different tale.

- With increasing medical advancements, we can expect to have a more quality and longer life in the future.

Chapter 6

HEALTH

The gift of long life and decreased mortality rates did not come to us from the heavens. The quality of human life has taken a giant leap forward since the 18th century. According to Angus Deaton, "ever since people rebelled against authority in the Enlightenment, and set about using the force of reason to make their lives better, they have found a way to do so, and there is little doubt that they will continue to win victories against the forces of death." Pinker concludes that longevity was achieved by successfully battling against the forces of disease, war, starvation, accidents, and homicide.

Infectious disease was among the most dreadful forces of death in the course of history. In earlier stages of society, *homo sapiens* frequently tried to ward off diseases and plagues with "quackery such as prayer, sacrifice, bloodletting, cupping, toxic metals, homeopathy, and squeezing a hen to death against an infected body part." But it was not until late in the 18th and during the 19th centuries that the tide of battle began to turn with the invention of vaccination and acceptance of the germ theory of disease, respectively. In addition, handwashing, midwifery, mosquito control, and especially the protection of drinking water by public sewerage and chlorinated tap water would come to save billions of lives." Karl Landsteiner alone saved *billions of lives* by discovering blood groups. Numerous other scientists helped save millions of lives with their major discoveries.

John Enders (1897–1985)	measles vaccine	120 million
Howard Florey (1898–1968)	penicillin	82 million
Gaston Ramon (1886–1963)	diphtheria and tetanus vaccines	60 million
David Nalin (1941–)	oral rehydration therapy	54 million
Paul Ehrlich (1854–1915)	diphtheria and tetanus antitoxins	42 million
Andreas Grüntzig (1939–1985)	angioplasty	15 million
Grace Eldering (1900–1988) and Pearl Kendrick (1890–1980)	whooping cough vaccine	14 million
Gertrude Elion (1918–1999)	rational drug design	5 million

According to the data gathered by various researchers, it is estimated that more than *five billion* lives have so far been saved by roughly the hundred scientists they selected.

More and more deadly diseases that wreaked havoc across planet have been obliterated and decimated during the past decades. For instance, "between 2000 and 2015, the number of deaths from malaria (which in the past killed half the people who had ever lived) fell by 60 percent." Since 1990s, infectious diseases have been under control, saving more than a hundred million children.

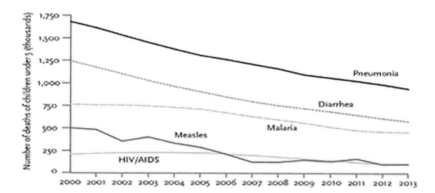

Figure 6-1: Childhood deaths from infectious disease, 2000–2013

Source: Child Health Epidemiology Reference Group of the World Health Organization, Liu et al. 2014, supplementary appendix.

Some of the most influential entrepreneurs and ex-presidents, such as Bill Gates, Jimmy Carter, Bill

Clinton, and George W. Bush made "their legacy the health of the poor in distant continents rather than glittering buildings close to home." Yet the greatest contributor was science, which not only provided effective medications but also *ideas* that may not have material value but they help save countless lives.

In Chapter 6 of his book, Steven Pinker discussed scientific advancements throughout history, which greatly reduced the amount of lives lost to numerous diseases:

- The quality of human life has significantly advanced since the 18th century.

- Karl Landsteiner saved *billions of lives* by discovering blood groups, and other scientists also helped save millions of lives with their major discoveries.

- Since 1990s, infectious diseases have been under control, which saved more than a hundred million children.

- Human reason, i.e., science, is the main facilitator of the quality life that we have today.

Chapter 7

SUSTENANCE

Evolution and entropy have condemned us to an ongoing need for energy. The *Bible* recounts seven lean years in Egypt and Famine as a horseman of the apocalypse. Even during the 19th century there were frequent crop failures which brought misery. The historian Fernand Braudel wrote that Europe before the 18th century endured famines every few decades. Today we live in the world where not few, but excessive calories are a major problem. The comedian Chris Rock observed that "this is the first society in history where the poor people are fat."

Recently, however, our world has enjoyed the little-noticed advance: the developing world has enough food to satisfy its needs. Pinker observes that this is "most obvious in China, whose 1.3 billion people now have access to an average of 3,100 calories per person per day, which according to US government guidelines, is the number needed by a highly active young man."

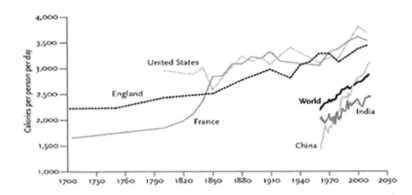

Figure 7-1: Calories, 1700-2013 (All rights reserved to the original book)

This figure shows a familiar pattern from earlier graphs: "hardships everywhere before the 19th century, rapid improvement in Europe and the United States over the next two centuries, and, in recent decades, the developing world catching up." One might think that rich people significantly boost the averages shown in Figure 7-1, but the values indicated in it include the bottom as well.

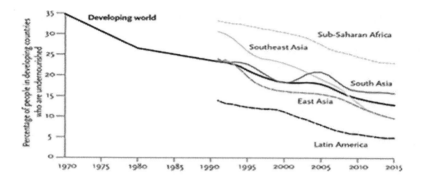

This figure shows the rate of undernourishment (a year or more of insufficient food) for developing countries in five regions and for the world as a whole. Pinker observes that "not only chronic undernourishment has been in decline, but so have catastrophic famines – the crises that kill people in large numbers and cause widespread wasting (the condition of being two standard deviations below one's expected weight) and kwashiorkor (the protein deficiency which causes swollen bellies)."

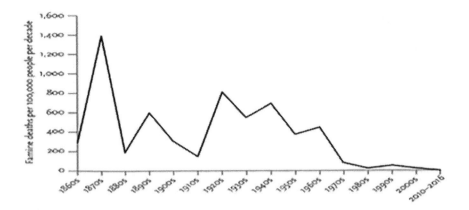

Figure 7-4: Famine deaths, 1860-2016 (All rights reserved to the original book)

We can observe in this graph that the trend has continued. Even though there is still hunger among the poor in developing countries, the famine tragedies from the past centuries will not happen again any time soon.

The Enlightenment and Industrial Revolution gave rise to major changes in food supply systems and economy. Huge scientific breakthroughs also played their part as well. Pinker states that in 1909 "Carl Bosch perfected a process invented by Fritz Haber which used methane and steam to pull nitrogen out of the air and turn it into fertilizer on an industrial scale." After 1950s the US agronomist, Norman Borlaug, prepared the ground for the Green Revolution. He "took evolution in his own hands, crossing thousands of strains of wheat" and evolving them "with many times the yield of their ancestors." With the help of the Green Revolution, the world today needs "less than a third of the land to produce a given amount of food."

In Chapter 7 of his book, Steven Pinker discussed some of the major advancements in overcoming famine and increasing food production on a global scale:

- Modern world has reached a stage in which major food crises have been reduced to a minimum.

- Rarely is it noted that our world has more than enough food to satisfy its demands.

- Figures show that undernourishment and famine deaths have developed an ongoing downward trend during the course of history.

- The Enlightenment, Industrial Revolution, and Green Revolution have enormously contributed to technological and other advancements in food production.

Chapter 8

WEALTH

The creation of wealth is often overshadowed by the discussions of its distribution. Economists and politicians frequently presuppose that wealth has been there all along. The realization that *wealth is created* originated in the Enlightenment. As Pinker indicates, "it is created primarily by knowledge and cooperation: networks of people arrange matter into improbable but useful configurations and combine the fruits of their ingenuity and labor. The corollary, just as radical, is that we can figure out how to make more of it."

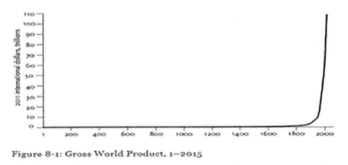

Figure 8-1: Gross World Product, 1–2015

Sources: Our World in Data, Roser 2016, based on data from the World Bank and from Angus Maddison and Maddison Project 2014.

This figure shows that after more than a millennium, the world's income experienced a great surge, tripling between 1820 and 1900, and again in a little more than fifty years, repeating the feat in the next thirty-three years. Pinker observes that "the Gross World Product today has grown almost a hundredfold since the Industrial Revolution was in place in 1820, and almost two hundredfold from the start of the Enlightenment in the 18th century."

We must attribute huge boosts in wealth during the nineteenth century and further to science, which lead to what the economic historian Joel Mokyr calls "the enlightened economy." The innovations such as the machines and factories of the Industrial Revolution, the water pipes of the Public Health Revolution, vehicles, tools, and other, cannot be imagined without two other great innovations. The first was "the development of *institutions* that lubricated the exchange of goods, services, and ideas. [...] Today I take it for granted that if I want some milk, I can walk into convenience store and a quart will be on the shelves, the milk won't be diluted or tainted, [...] and the owner will let me walk out with it after a swipe of a card, even though we have never met." The second innovation was a change in values. For instance, the 18th century French philosopher Voltaire praised the spirit of commerce for being able to rise above sectarian hatreds. The historian Roy Porter has noticed that "the Enlightenment thus translated the ultimate question 'How can I be saved?' into the pragmatic 'How can I be happy' – thereby heralding a new praxis of personal and social adjustment." Apart from Great Britain and the Netherlands, the "Great Escape" from poverty has been achieved by the Germanic states, Nordic countries, as well as Australia, New Zealand, Canada, and the US.

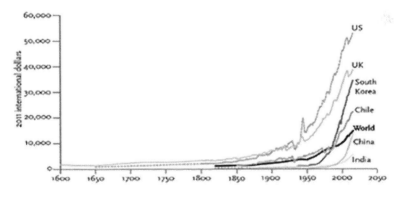

Figure 8-2: GDP per capita, 1600–2015

Source: *Our World in Data*. Roser 2016c, based on data from the World Bank and from Maddison Project 2014.

(All rights reserved to the original book)

This figure displays another astonishing chapter in the history of prosperity. This one started in the late 20th century and during that time many poor countries have been escaping poverty in turns. Pinker notes that diverse developing countries, such as "Bangladesh, El Salvador, Ethiopia, Georgia, Mongolia, Mozambique, Panama, Rwanda, Uzbekistan, and Vietnam have enjoyed economic growth rates that amount to doubling of income every eighteenth years." It is evident that extreme poverty is being eradicated and the world is becoming middle class.

In Chapter 8 of his study, Steven Pinker reflected on advancements in global economy and accumulation of wealth:

- The idea that *wealth is created* originated in the Enlightenment.

- Data indicate that after more than a millennium, the world's income has experienced a great surge.

- Great economic advancements in the 19th century must be attributed to science.

- The Gross World Product today has grown almost a hundredfold since the Industrial Revolution in 1820.

- Numerous developing countries have boosted their economy and caught up to western economic leaders, such as Great Britain and the US.

- Large famine crises have been eradicated and the world is becoming middle class.

Chapter 9

INEQUALITY

E conomic inequality has become a 21st century obsession. Pope Francis called it "the root of social evil," Barack Obama "the defining challenge of our time." Obviously, the economic surplus described in the previous chapter does not contribute to the overall human welfare anymore. A signature of the left, economic inequality became prominent following the Great Recession in 2007. A large number of people interpret this apparent inequality as a sign modernity's failed attempt to improve the human condition.

The fundamental point for understanding this issue is that income (in)equality is not among central components of well-being. Far more important are health, prosperity, knowledge, safety, and peace. As the philosopher Harry Frankfurt wrote, "from the point of view of morality, it is not important everyone should have the *same*. What is morally important is that each should have *enough*." Discussions of inequality often bring up another common confusion: the confusion of inequality with fairness. With regard to that occurrence, some psychologists have posited a syndrome called inequality aversion – their desire the wealth to be shared equally. Other psychologists, such as Christina Starmans and Mark Sheskin, claim that people actually prefer *unequal* distributions, as long as they are *fair*. Therefore, Pinker concludes that "narratives about the *causes* of inequality loom larger in people's minds than the *existence* of inequality."

The common narrative regarding inequality is that it came with modernity. According to this story, inequality started at zero. With increased wealth over time, inequality increased. Pinker observes that "sedentary hunter-gatherers, such as the natives of the Pacific Northwest, which is flush with salmon, berries, and fur-bearing animals, were florid inegalitarians, and developed a hereditary nobility who kept slaves, hoarded luxuries, and flaunted their wealth in gaudy potlaches."

In the previous chapter certain graphs showed that developing countries started to catch up to their developed counterparts. Therefore, we saw hints of a global inequality decline in the blastoff of GDP in Asian countries. This brings us to a proposition that poor countries are getting richer faster than the rich countries, which can be shown by using an international Gini (inequality measurement), which treats each country as a person.

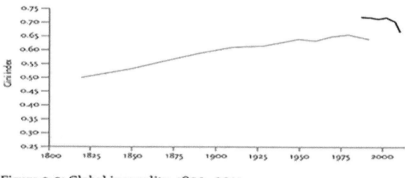

Figure 9-2: Global inequality, 1820–2011

Source: Milanović 2016, fig. 3-1. The left-hand curve shows 1990 international dollars of disposable income per capita; the right-hand curve shows 2005 international dollars, and combines household surveys of per capita disposable income and consumption.

The international and global Gini curves display that *inequality in the world is declining*, in spite of the rising anxiety about inequality in Western countries. What is specific about this particular inequality decline is that it is a decline in poverty.

Critics of modern society often remark that today's capitalist societies show no sympathy for the poor. However, they are unaware of the fact that a much smaller proportion of wealth was spent on the poor from the Renaissance through the early 20th century. There are countries and period in which there was spent nothing at all. A recent example of progress (aka the Egalitarian Revolution), as Pinker notices, shows that "modern societies now devote a substantial chunk of their wealth to health, education, pensions, and income support."

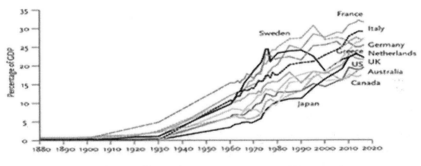

Figure 9-4: Social spending, OECD countries, 1880–2016

The figure shows that social spending surged during middle decades of the 20th century. "Social spending now takes up a median of 22 percent of their GDP.

Social spending may not be designed to reduce inequality, but that is certainly one of its effects.

The data displayed in this and previous chapter counters the common criticism that in modern society only rich people have prospered whereas everyone else has been stagnating or suffering. Certainly, this claim is false for the world *as a whole*, because the majority of humans has become much better off. Of course, the rich have prospered more than the rest, but the claim about the rest is not true. Globalization and technology combined have transformed what is usually taken to mean a poor person. Pinker claims that "today, the poor are likely to be as overweight as their employers, and dressed in the same fleece, sneakers, and jeans." Therefore, the long-term trend in history has shown that the Enlightenment ideals proved beneficial for everyone. Aside from having generated huge amounts of money, contemporary societies have devoted a large part of their wealth to poorer groups.

In Chapter 9 of his book, Steven Pinker provided an in-depth analysis on inequality, which is often emphasized by critics as the woe of modern society:

- Many people misinterpret inequality as modernity's failed attempt to improve the human condition.

- Inequality is not a central component of human well-being.

- Inequality is often confused to be a lack of fairness in our society.

- In recent history, inequality has been on a decline as developing countries' economies took off.

- Despite the usual claims, modern societies have devoted a substantial amount of their wealth to help the poor.

- Globalization and technology have transformed what is usually meant by a poor person.

Chapter 10

THE ENVIRONMENT

The usual criticism of the world today is that good news won't last long. If all the negative processes, such as overpopulation, resource depletion, and pollution, don't finish us off, the climate change will. Pinker's key idea, as in previous chapters, is that environmental problems, like any other, can be solved with the right knowledge.

The global scientific awareness of environmental problems increased from 1960s onwards due to breakthroughs in ecology, public health, as well as earth and atmospheric sciences. The increasing interest gradually grew into a movement that made the health of the planet its permanent agenda. However, the start of 1970s gave birth to greenism, a quasi-religious ideology whose supporters believed that the Earth is a green safe haven defiled by human material and technological rise. Recently, a counter-approach to environmental protection was set into motion, known as Ecomodernism, Ecopragmatism, or Enlightenment Environmentalism.

Ecomodernists realized that a certain degree of pollution cannot be avoided due to the Second Law of Thermodynamics. In other words, when people use energy for their bodies and homes, they increase entropy elsewhere in the environment as waste, pollution, etc. Contrary to the popular belief, Ecomodernists also realized that industrialization has been beneficial to humanity. As Pinker maintains, "it has fed billions, doubled life spans, slashed extreme poverty, and, by replacing muscle with machinery, made it easier to end slavery, emancipate women, and educate children [...] Any costs in pollution and habitat loss have to be weighted against these gifts." Furthermore, developing countries may prioritize economic development to environment. But when they reach the "developed" status, environment will arouse their interest due pressure from public activists. Let us not forget that technological advancements benefit humanity. Today, environmental problems are among technology's primary focuses.

Modern civilization skeptics have prophesized many apocalyptic scenarios for our planet. One of them was that the planet will become overpopulated. But that doesn't mean birthrates have multiplied. More likely, deaths have been considerably reduced.

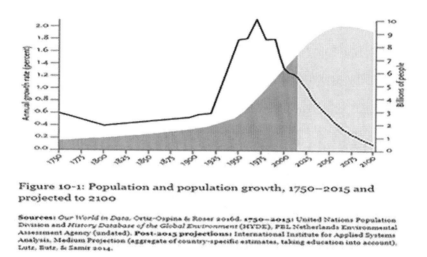

Figure 10-1: Population and population growth, 1750–2015 and projected to 2100

Sources: *Our World in Data*. Ortiz-Ospina & Roser 2016d. 1750–2015: United Nations Population Division and *History Database of the Global Environment* (HYDE), PBL Netherlands Environmental Assessment Agency (undated). Post-2015 projections: International Institute for Applied Systems Analysis, Medium Projection (aggregate of country-specific estimates, taking education into account), Lutz, Butz, & Samir 2014.

According to this figure, global population growth rate reached its peak at 2.1 percent a year in 1962. By 2010, it fell to 1.2 percent, and is projected to fall to less than 0.5 percent by 2050.

Another apocalyptic scenario was that the world would deplete its resources. The 1972 bestseller *The Limits to Growth* projected that the world will exhaust its supplies of copper, zinc, gold, chromium, nickel, etc.

But that did not come to pass. Common thinking that humans will simply suck resources from the earth has proven wrong time and time again. Another fallacy is to think that we need recourses in the first place. People *need* food growing methods, traveling, lighting their homes. Such needs are satisfied with ideas: formulas, recipes, blueprints, and techniques that help them use the outside world to suit their own well-being. People usually think that our civilization urgently need to acquire new resources before old ones are exhausted. Truth is, "societies have always abandoned a resource for a better one long before the old one was exhausted."

Instead of prophesized apocalypses, various improvements that were never imagined took place. Since 1970, when the Environmental Protection Agency was formed, the US has cut down its five air pollutants by almost two-thirds. Energy use has declined and carbon dioxide emissions have leveled off. Such declines reflect improved efficiency and emission control. Also, deforestation of Amazon, the world's largest tropical forest, peaked in 1995 and in the next 18 years its rate fell by four-fifths. The peak of environmental insults are oil spills from tankers that supposedly cover pristine beaches with toxic sludge.

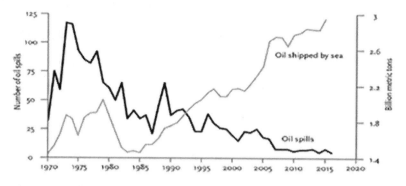

Figure 10-5: Oil spills, 1970–2016

(All rights reserved to the original book)

The graph displays rise in oil shipped and declining trend in oil spills. Of course, people more often remember accidents than vast improvements. Pinker emphasizes that such important improvements do not mean that the environment takes care of itself. The cleaner environment of today is largely due to legislation, activism, arguments, treaties, regulations, and technological ingenuity from those who tried to improve out environment in the past. Instead of listening to narratives about the need to abandon technology, we ought to understand environmental protection as a challenge that we face and a question to tackle: how can we live comfortable, safe, and stimulating lives with the least possible pollution of our natural habitat? Such complex questions push us to strive for more. They are the key component of humankind's continuous progress.

In Chapter 10 of his book, Steven Pinker discussed common environmental issues and pointed to numerous advances in safeguarding the environment:

- Right knowledge and ideas are the key that can solve, among others, any environmental problem.

- As opposed to growing pessimism in the latter half of the 20th century, a counter approach called Ecomodernism arose to address solutions to various environmental issues.

- Modern skeptics of our civilization talked about different apocalyptic scenarios, such as pollution and resource depletion, but none of this happened.

- Civilization is constantly finding alternative resources to satisfy all energy demands.

- Environment does not safeguard itself. We must continue to battle entropy and negative effects in order to continue progressing.

- Dealing with the challenges of keeping the environment and ourselves safe is what fuels human desire toward progress.

Chapter 11

PEACE

In his book *The Better Angels of Our Nature* (2011), Steven Pinker showed that since the first half of the 21st century, every objective measure of violence has slowly declined. In this chapter, the author attempts to show that since the publication of his 2011 book, an ongoing trend of peace took place, instead of widely prophesized armed conflicts on a global scale, nuclear crises, and other popular movie forms of violence.

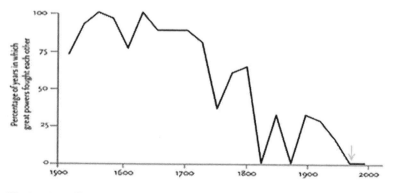

Figure 11-1: Great power war, 1500–2015

Source: Levy & Thompson 2011, updated for the 21st century. Percentage of years the great powers fought each other in wars, aggregated over 25-year periods, except for 2000–2015. The arrow points to 1975–1999, the last quarter-century plotted in fig. 5–12 of Pinker 2011.

This figure shows that great powers were constantly at war, but nowadays they are never at war. Today it seems war in the classic sense of a large armed conflict between two countries has become obsolete. Pinker observes that "there have been no more than three [wars] in any year since 1945, none in most years since 1989, and none since the American-led invasion of Iraq in 2003." Our world has entered a period now known as the Long Peace. But this doesn't mean that war is impossible, but it is surely something that nations avoid at all costs. However, the geography of war has noticeably reduced. Western Europe's centuries of warfare have stopped and allowed more than seven decades of peace, East and Southeast Asia are today almost completely free from interstate conflicts, to name but a few cases. Of course, there are still conflicts in a zone from Nigeria to Pakistan, but this area contains less than a sixth of the world's population. Apart from conflicts driven by a radical Islamist group and the Syrian civil war, there hasn't been an increase in the number of wars. The civil war in Syria, with battle deaths counting 250,000 (as of

2016), there hasn't been larger upticks in war deaths on a global level.

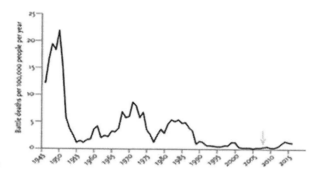

Figure 11-2: Battle deaths, 1946–2016

Numerous people assert that the world has learned little from the Holocaust, the truth is different. We have witnessed nothing similar to the blood flood of the 1940s. But war statistics don't tell the whole tale. We need to supply numbers with theoretical knowledge. UNESCO motto states that "War begins in the minds of men." Indeed, the turn away from war is not only reflected in a reduced number of armed conflicts or deaths. It is also the prevalence of conscription and the size of military forces.

During the Enlightenment and the Age of Reason, famous people such as Swift, Voltaire, Pascal, Samuel Johnson, and others denounced war. Practical suggestions on how to eliminate war appeared in Kant's essay "Perpetual Peace." But only after World War II have these suggestions been put into practice. Today, *war is illegal*; "the world's nations have committed themselves to not waging war except in self-defense or with the approval of the United Nations Security Council.

Pinker identifies the origins of a war-endorsing narrative during the age of military Romanticism, when writers and philosophers such as Alexis de Tocqueville, Emil Zola, and Hegel though that war was necessary to preserve identity of a nation. This is opposite to the Enlightenment-inspired idea of problem-solving. Some people blindly insist that an insatiable desire for conquest is in human nature. However, notions such as democracy, trade, economic development, and international norms have helped maintain peace in the world.

In Chapter 11 of his book, Steven Pinker discussed the notion of war and how it declined after World War II:

- In *The Better Angels of Our Nature* (2011), Steven Pinker showed that violence declined since the first half of the 21st century.

- Today a large part of the world enjoys the period known as the Long Peace.

- Throughout history, great powers used to be constantly at war, but nowadays they are never.

- During the Enlightenment, many thinkers denounced war. Immanuel Kant gave practical solutions on how to exterminate wars in his essay "Perpetual Peace."

- The nationalistic idea that war is necessary for a country originated in military Romanticism.

- Economic development, democracy, global trade, and international norms have been keeping the peace.

Chapter 12

SAFETY

There are countless ways human safety can be compromised. Our ancestors from the distant past lived in constant danger of predators such as crocodiles, snakes, and large cats. Nowadays various diseases and accidents take many lives. Human knowledge of how death or severe injury are caused is today beyond anything religious. According to Pinker, "we are now living in the safest time in history."

Centuries ago, in medieval Europe, more people were killed on roads by highwaymen and brigands, died in duels while fighting each other, or were stabbed over insults. Norbert Elias, German sociologist, claims that in the 14th century, people began to resolve their disputes in less violent ways. He asserts that centralized kingdoms were the main cause of this change. Another fundamental change occurred in the

19th century, when more deliberative legal systems and municipal police forces were implemented.

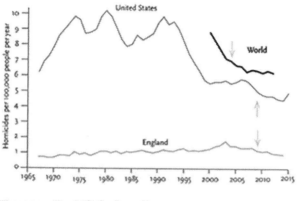

Figure 12-2: Homicide deaths, 1967–2015

The figure shows that beginning in 1992, the US homicide rate plummeted, and then dived again in 2007, during the Great Recession. Canada, England, and most other industrialized countries experienced fall in homicide rates as well.

Violence is a recurring problem, but that doesn't mean it cannot be solved. First, effective law enforcement has to be implemented. The upper left peaks of the curve in figure 12-2 is due to ineffective law enforcement systems. Eisner provided a sensible suggestion on how to reduce the homicide rate: "An effective rule of law, based on legitimate law enforcement, victim protection, swift and fair adjudication, moderate punishment, and humane prisons is critical to sustainable reductions in lethal violence." Aside from effective law enforcement, the *legitimate* regime is also important for secure society.

Humans rarely appreciate the conquest of everyday danger as a form of progress. Accidents kill more people than wars, but people always say "accidents will happen." If they are not the victims, people do not tend to observe accidents as atrocities. Thus, they don't see that wins in safety are moral triumphs as well. However, sparing countless lives and sufferings certainly deserve our gratitude and respect.

In Chapter 12 of his book, Steven Pinker provided a detailed analysis of improved safety on a global scale:

- Human safety can be endangered in numerous ways.

- Advances in securing safety can only be attributed to human reason and science.

- Lower homicide rates testify to improved legal systems in developed states.

- Effective law enforcement and a legitimate regime are the necessary components of a safe society.

- Accidents kill more people than wars.

Chapter 13

TERRORISM

According to most recent polls on the safety in the US, terrorism was voted as the critical issue which the country faces. Recently, terrorist attacks have been highly publicized. They fostered an illusion that we are living in exceedingly dangerous times. Even John Grey, a known political philosopher, stated that we are surrounded by "terrains of violent conflict" in which "peace and war are fatally blurred."

All of this is an illusion as terrorism distracts our progress. The danger of terrorism is somewhat higher in Western Europe than in the United States. In 2015, there were registered attacks in the Brussels airport, a few nightclubs in Paris, and a public celebration in Nice (in 2014, only five people were killed in the attacks). United States and Europe both account for a tenth of the world's population, yet in 2015 they suffered one-half of one percent of deaths from terrorist attacks. Also, not many people notice that the majority of global deaths from terrorist attacks happen in civil war zones, such as Iraq, Afghanistan, Nigeria, Syria, Pakistan, and Libya.

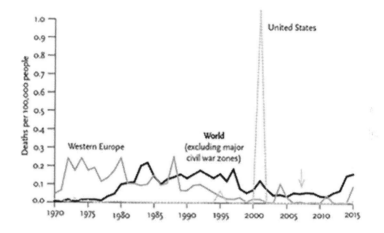

Figure 13-1: Terrorism deaths, 1970–2015

"Terrorism" is an elastic category and it is not easily measured. Therefore, following historical trends for this category is difficult. "Shooter" incidents have risen in the US since 2000, but "mass murders" (more than four deaths in an incident) shows a decline from 1976 to 2011. Three thousand deaths rate from 9/11 attacks as well as Oklahoma bombing in 1995 dominate the graph in Figure 13-1.

The data indicates that terrorist poses a minor danger as compared to other risks, but it causes mass panic, which is precisely its aim. Thanks to overblown media coverages, people are thrown into panic and fear that are disproportionate to the actual level of danger. We must ask ourselves whether it is *rational* to worry so much about terrorism, when the amount of damage they do is small? Terrorist violence strikes victims at random. Their primary aim is to spread fear and panic, and to send a message. Terrorism has certainly risen in public eyes, but it is not a sign that the world has become dangerous. Political scientists such as Audrey Cronin, Virginia Page Fortna, and Max Abrahms conducted surveys and found that since the 1960s, all terrorist actions were extinguished without achieving their strategic aims.

In Chapter 13 of his book, Steven Pinker discussed the popular topic of terrorism and indicated that the growing fear of terrorist attacks is totally unfounded:

- Recent terrorist attacks created the illusion that we are living in highly dangerous times.

- Most terrorist actions and deaths resulting from them happen in countries struck by civil war.

- There were many "shooter" incidents in the United States, but fewer "mass" deaths.

- The primary strategic aim of terrorist attacks is to spread fear and panic.

- Overblown media coverages regarding terrorism does not reflect the actual level of danger it poses.

Chapter 14

DEMOCRACY

Democracy is among the primary indicators of progress in modern world. It is a form of government that allows people to pursue their happiness in safety from violence and tyranny. That is one of the reasons why democracy heavily contributes to human flourishing. In addition, democracy enables exponential economic growth, fewer wars, educated and healthier citizens, and almost no famines. Pinker concludes that "if the world has become more democratic over time, that is progress."

Samuel Huntington, political scientist, outlined three waves within the history of democracy. The first was in the 19th century, when the US constitutional democracy came into effect. It lasted until fascism pushed it back in 1942. The second wave gathered following the defeat of fascism after World War II, when European colonies gained independence. By

1962 there were 36 recognized democratic societies. However, democracy was sandwiched between imperial Russia in the east and fascist Spain and Portugal in the southwest. Many politicians and senators, such as Willy Brandt and Daniel Patrick Moynihan, thought that democracy was a thing of the past. However, the third democratic wave erupted when fascist and military governments in Greece, Spain, and Portugal fell in 1974, 1975, and 1976, respectively. The Berlin Wall crumbled in 1989, allowing east-European nations to create democratic governments. With the fall of Russian communism in 1991, Russia and many other countries made the transition to democracy. In his famous 1989 essay, political scientist Francis Fukuyama stated that liberal democracy was "the end of history."

When compared to autocracy, a form of government which still endures to some extent in countries such as Turkey and Russia, democracy prevails.

Figure 14-1: Democracy versus autocracy, 1800-2015

Source: HumanProgress. http://humanprogress.org/f1/1360, based on *Polity IV Annual Time-Series,* 1800-2015. Marshall, Gurr, & Jaggers 2016. Scores are summed over sovereign states with a population greater than 500,000, and range from -10 for a complete autocracy to 10 for a perfect democracy. The arrow points to 2008, the last year plotted in fig. 5-23 of Pinker 2011.

The graph indicates that the third wave of democracy will not be soon over, even though its rise is not equal to the years around the fall of the Berlin Wall. Even though it is not the end of history, democracy is more attractive than ever.

Democracy should not be evaluated by voting. When in office, politicians vote the position of their party no matter what the opinion of their constituents is. But in his 1945 book *The Open Society and its Enemies,* philosopher Karl Popper posited that democracy should not be understood as an answer to the question "Who should rule?" but as a way of stopping bad leadership and bloodshed. Political scientist John

Mueller suggest that the essence of democracy is to allow people the freedom to complain: "It comes about when the people effectively agree not to use violence to replace the leadership, and the leadership leaves them free to try to dislodge it by any other means."

In Chapter 14 of his book, Steven Pinker discussed the concept of *democracy* and how closely it is related to the idea of progress:

- Democracy is an indicator of progress in the modern world. It is a form of government which allows people to freely pursue their happiness.

- Samuel Huntington outlined three waves in the history of democracy from the end of the World War II to the fall of the Berlin Wall in 1989.

- Francis Fukuyama famously stated that liberal democracy was the end of history.

- If states have advanced in democracy, they have also achieved progress.

Chapter 15

Equal Rights

Phenomena such as racism, sexism, and homophobia have dominated most cultures throughout the course of history. Rejecting these evils is today understood as equal rights or civil rights – a necessary prerequisite for any progressive society. In 2017 we witnessed the completion of two terms in office by Barack Obama, the first African American president. He was succeeded by the first woman nominee in a presidential election.

But the belief in progress was challenged when in our recent history where, during his campaign, Donald Trump shouted anti-Muslim, anti-Hispanic, and misogynistic insults. Some analysts were worried that his presidency represented a failure of the nation's path to equal rights. There have been questions whether we had made any progress in the first place.

Are equal rights an illusion if they can easily change their course backwards?

We have seen that data and graphs from previous chapters speak in favor of the idea of progress. The Pew Research center has conducted a research to find out Americans' thoughts on gender, race, and sexual orientation over the past quarter century. The results of this research testify that people's attitudes towards these subjects have experienced a "fundamental shift" towards human rights.

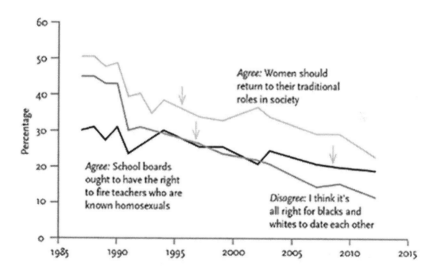

Figure 15-1: Racist, sexist, and homophobic opinions, US, 1987–2012

Source: Pew Research Center 2012b. The arrows point to the most recent years plotted in Pinker 2011 for similar questions: Blacks, 1997 (fig. 7–7); Women, 1995 (fig. 7–11); Homosexuals, 2009 (fig. 7–24).

The graph indicates an obvious decline in prejudice, with a smaller number of people who would admit their true opinion to a pollster.

The economist Seth Stephens-Davidowitz conducted researches of the Google search results about racial bigoted jokes. His results indicated that such searches were common in the areas of older and less educated parts of the country. Observing the results further, he concluded that private prejudice was declining with time and youth. This indicates that a further decline can be expected as younger generations succeed older ones.

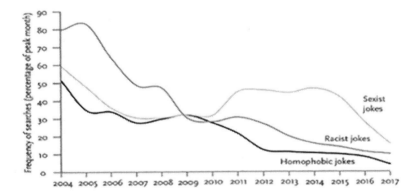

Figure 15-2: Racist, sexist, and homophobic Web searches, US, 2004–2017

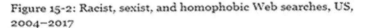

Source: Google Trends (www.google.com/trends), searches for "nigger jokes," "bitch jokes," and "fag jokes," United States, 2004–2017, relative to total search volume. Data (accessed Jan. 22, 2017) are by month, expressed as a percentage of the peak month for each search term, then averaged over the months of each year, and smoothed.

In addition, Pinker reports declines in poverty among African American population (from 55 percent in 1960 to 27.6 percent in 2011), a rise of life expectancy (from 33 in 1900 to 75.6 years in 2015, and illiteracy rate decline among African Americans (from 45 percent in 1900 to zero percent today). Further research indicates that crime against Jewish, whites, and Asian targets has fallen as well.

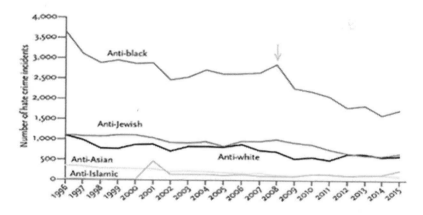

Figure 15-3: Hate crimes, US, 1996–2015

Source: Federal Bureau of Investigation 2016b. The arrow points to 2008, the last year plotted in fig. 7–4 of Pinker 2011.

In Chapter 15 of his monograph, Steven Pinker analyzed the subject of equal rights and provided statistical analyses that show various advancements in acknowledging civil and human rights:

- The concept of equal rights is an important factor in the progress of any modern state.

- Research indicates that there has been a fundamental shift in people's attitude toward equality.

- A further decline in attitude towards equal rights can be expected as younger generations succeed older ones.

- Pinker reported advancements in the decline of poverty, crime, and illiteracy among African Americans.

Chapter 16

KNOWLEDGE

Ever since the first hunter-gatherers, human knowledge was continually expanding. Today, knowledge redefines our place in the world; it broadens the understanding of who we are, where we came from, and how the world works. Throughout history, schools were at times accused of spreading religious or patriotic wisdom. The educational theorist George Counts states that "with the coming of modern age, formal education assumed a significance far in excess of anything that the world had yet seen. [...] The school expanded horizontally and vertically until it took its place along with the state, the church, the family and property as one of society's most powerful institutions."

The benefits of education for any country's progress are numerous. Studies have shown that education makes countries richer, more democratic and peaceful. They have confirmed that educated people are more enlightened, i.e., less racist, xenophobic, sexist, homophobic, and authoritarian. Educated people are more likely to volunteer, vote, join civic associations, and voice political opinions. For all these reasons, education is certainly among the most crucial components of any civilized society. Education's foundation, literacy, doubled in the 20th century and quadrupled in the 21st. Today, 83 percent of the world is literate.

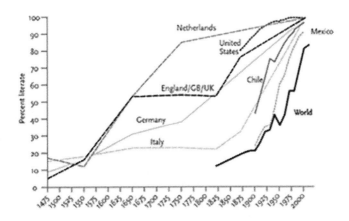

Figure 16-1: Literacy, 1475–2010

Source: Our World in Data, Roser & Ortiz-Ospina 2016b, including data from the following. Before 1800: Buringh & Van Zanden 2009. World: van Zanden et al. 2014. US: National Center for Education Statistics. After 2000: Central Intelligence Agency 2016.

Researches project that by the end of this century, the number of uneducated population will fall to zero.

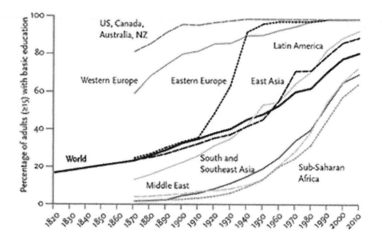

Figure 16-2: Basic education, 1820-2010

Source: *Our World in Data*, Roser & Nagdy 2016c, based on data from van Zanden et al. 2014. The graphs indicate the share of the population aged 15 or older that had completed at least a year of education (more in later eras); see van Leeuwen & van Leeuwen-Li 2014, pp. 88-93.

As basic education sores in almost every country, so does the number of years spent in education, which has extended into tertiary and postgraduate education in universities and colleges. In 1920, only 28 percent of American children ages 14 to 17 were attending high school. By 2011 80 percent graduated and 70 percent of them continued their education on college. But does more educated people also mean smarter people? Have people become adept at solving more problems, acquiring more skills, and grasping critical thinking? Most people would probably say no, but IQ scores have been rising for more than a century in every part of the world.

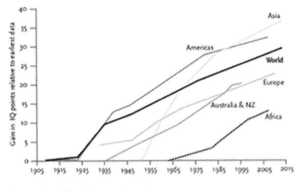

Figure 16-5: IQ gains, 1909–2013

Source: Pietschnig & Voracek 2015, supplemental online material. The lines display changes in IQ measured by different tests starting at different times and cannot be compared with one another.

Some researches have been skeptical whether the 20th century really produced more fascinating ideas than the age of Hume and Goethe. But let us not forget that brilliant minds of the past centuries had a vast territory of unexplored ideas at their exposal. As Pinker observes, "today the intellectual landscape is well trodden, and it's harder for a solitary genius to tower above the crowd of hypereducated and networked thinkers who are mapping every nook and cranny."

The United Nations Development Programme came up with the unique measure of progress – the Human Development Index that includes three major ones: life expectancy, education, and GDP per capita (health, wisdom, and wealth).

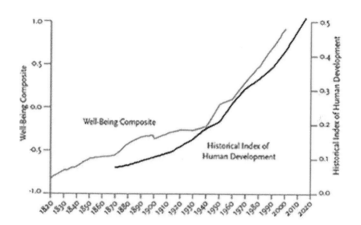

Figure 16-6: Global well-being, 1820–2015

Sources: Historical Index of Human Development: Prados de la Escosura 2015, 0–1 scale, available at Our World in Data. Roser 2016b. Well-Being Composite: Rijpma 2014, p. 259, standard deviation scale over country-decades.

This graph allows us to behold the rise of human progress. Even though the world remains unequal, each region has been improving.

In Chapter 16 of his book, Steven Pinker emphasized the concepts of knowledge and education for human progress:

- Since the very first humans, knowledge has been expanding.

- Studies have shown that education makes countries richer, more democratic and peaceful.

- Today, 83 percent of people in the world are literate.

- Researchers project that by the end of the 21st century there will be no uneducated people in the world.

- The United Nations Development Programme has indicated that human progress (measured by education, GDP, and health) is continuously rising.

Chapter 17

QUALITY OF LIFE

Health and affluence are not the only components of a quality life. Seemingly a simple concept, life is much more complex than that. Martha Nussbaum, the philosopher, has provided a set of "fundamental capabilities" of an average human being. These are the already discussed concepts of health, literacy, safety, knowledge, free expression, and political participation. However, she also adds recreation and play, aesthetic experience, emotional attachments, social affiliations, enjoyment of nature, and reflecting on one's one conception of the good life.

Modernity allows people to exercise all of these capabilities, which brings to notion of a quality life even higher, beyond the economic metrics such as wealth and longevity. Thus, the ultimate form of progress includes the ability to enjoy intellectual, social, aesthetic, natural, and cultural wonders of the world. God of the Hebrew Bible proclaimed that "in the sweat of thy face shalt thou eat bread," and for the majority of history, this is how it was. But modernity has brought us fewer working hours, despite what some may think.

Figure 17-1: Work hours, Western Europe and US, 1870–2000

Source: Roser 2016, based on data from Huberman & Minns 2007 on full-time production workers (both sexes) in nonagricultural activities.

The figure shows that in 1870s people in the Western Europe had an average of 66 working hours per week, whereas an average American had 62. Over the past century and a half, employees have been spared from such a workload and gained 28 fewer hours a week (22 hours in the US). As Morgan Housel put it, "we constantly worry about the looming 'retirement funding crisis' in America without realizing that the entire concept of retirement is unique to the last five decades. It wasn't long ago that the average American man had two stages of life: work and death [...] Think of it this way: The average American now retires at age 62. One hundred years ago, the average American died at age 51."

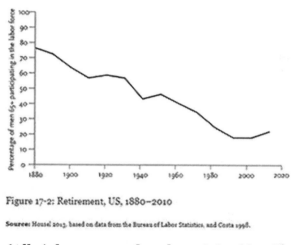

Figure 17-2: Retirement, US, 1880–2010

Source: Housel 2013, based on data from the Bureau of Labor Statistics, and Costa 1998.

The figure shows that almost 80 percent of Americans in 1880 were still working, even though by today's standards they should have retired. This number had fallen to less than 20 percent by 1990. In the past, workers were worried not to get sick and be replaced, but nowadays senior citizens than their younger counterparts at working age. Also, another pipe dream became a reality: paid vacation. Today an average US employee with five years on the job receives six more years (22) than in 1970 (16). Of course, these are the trends which favor the West, but as developing countries get richer, they would soon follow suit.

Obviously, there can be no doubt about which era was the most prosperous. The answer would be "today," and after that "tomorrow." At our fingertips are basically all the genius works from past eras. The global cultural heritage is available to anyone who is connected to the great web of knowledge, which means we have the whole of humanity at our disposal.

In Chapter 17 of his book, Steven Pinker discussed how quality of life today is incomparably better to those of previous eras:

- Being rich and healthy are not the most important things in life.

- The fundamental capabilities of an average human include enjoying intellectual, social, aesthetic, natural, and cultural wonders of the world.

- The ultimate form of progress is realizing that man is able to enjoy these wonders.

- Modernity has brought us fewer working hours, paid vacations, and earlier retirement.

- Our era is certainly the most prosperous in history, and it can only get better.

Chapter 18

HAPPINESS

All things considered so far, we ought to be happier if we had but a tiny shred of gratitude. But data says we are not, if popular impressions are a guide. People always seem to complain about this and that. They are either blind or fed up with the progress of modernity (how can one be fed up with something positive?). In 1999, John Mueller summarized the common understanding of modernity: "People seem simply to have taken a remarkable economic improvement in stride and have deftly found new concerns to get upset about. In an important sense, then, things never get better." This is called the Easterlin paradox, and two theories in psychology were proposed to explain it. First, there is a theory of the hedonic treadmill, according to which people adapt to changes in their life, like our eyes adapt to light and darkness, and quickly return to their genetically predetermined baseline. The second is the theory of social comparison, according to which they measure happiness by how pleased they are in comparison with their compatriots. Therefore, if a country gets richer but more unequal, people may feel worse.

In 2016, George Monbiot, an activist, attacked the cultural pessimism's campaign against modernity. His tag line was, "Epidemics of mental illness are crushing the minds and bodies of millions. It's time to ask where we are heading and why." If we think that all those years of modernity and progress have left us despondent with depression, anxiety, higher suicide rates, etc., then we ought to think whether history has played the greatest joke on humanity? We need to face the facts about human progress and observe things from a different perspective.

First of all, we have to realize that freedom has inherent value and has been crucial for the progress of humankind. Along with life and reason, freedom is a prerequisite for evaluating what is good. If we lament the direction of our civilization, then we have already chosen our path. Happiness has two sides: emotional and cognitive. The first consists of a balance between positive emotions such as joy, elation, delight, and pride, whereas negative consists of emotions such as anger, worry, and sadness. Since there are no exact measurements of these concepts, we have to rely on people's own estimations of how they feel. Numerous aspects of life can affect people's answer to this difficult question, such as their current mood, weather, etc. The paradox is that there is no perfect life without anxiety and sadness, which introduces the final aspect of a good life: meaning and purpose. Some long-term goals, such as raising a family or writing a book may leave us worried and unhappy for some time, but their fulfillment can be a worthy cause.

We have to agree that citizens in developed countries are not as happy as they should be, given all the progress and prosperity which are ongoing. Of course, adults have their own ways of evaluating life, with all its worry and sadness. But a little anxiety is not such a bad thing if it motivates people to support solutions to bigger problems.

In Chapter 18 of his book, Steven Pinker analyzed the concept of happiness. He concluded that happiness does not depend solely on wealth and being healthy:

- Considering how our civilization progressed, we should be happier.

- Happiness is among the major life components of an adult man and cannot be imagined without worry and anxiety.

- An important factor for happiness is *freedom*, which allows us to evaluate our lives the way we see fit.

- Anxiety can be good if it motivates people to solve problems and progress.

Chapter 19

EXISTENTIAL THREATS

The more our world is climbing the ladder of progress, the more people talk about existential threats. The so-called four horsemen of the apocalypse (overpopulation, resource depletion, pollution, and nuclear war) have already been discussed in previous chapters. This book, however, does not prophesize that apocalypse is an impossible scenario. While some threats are merely an imagination, there are others which are genuine. But we should not treat them as apocalypses, but problems that can be solved.

Recent polls have stated that 15 percent of the people worldwide are troubled about the current state of the world. But how should we regard catastrophic threats? The fate of our species is the most pertinent question of all. Technology experts usually claim that our civilization will determine its own grim fate. But this tech-apocalyptic claim that our civilization will destroy itself is ill-conceived. Sure, most civilizations throughout history were destroyed. However, David Deutsch emphasized that these civilizations could have averted their fate if they had better medical, agricultural, or military technology.

Among the most popular "dangers" of the 21st century is the artificial intelligence (AI), sometimes called the Robopocalypse. The reality behind this concept is that it owes more to the Great Chain of Being and the Nietzschean will to power than a valid scientific understanding. Pinker observes the narrative behind this supposedly apocalyptic scenario: "Since we humans have used our moderate endowment to domesticate or exterminate less well-endowed animals (and since technologically advanced societies have enslaved or annihilate technologically primitive ones), it follows that supersmart AI would do the same to us." But there is an inherent fallacy in this type of reasoning. We must not confuse intelligence with wanting or motivation. Even if there were super intelligent robots, why would they want to enslave their masters? Secondly, intelligence is not about 'wanting' something, but about deploying novel means to attain a goal. No wonder numerous AI researchers are annoyed by those who claim that General Artificial Intelligence is just around the corner. Advances in AI have not come from a broader understanding but from larger data and faster chips.

Another phantom menace may be bioterrorism. However, bioweapons did not play any role in modern warfare. In 1972, they were renounced by virtually every nation in an international convention. Biological weapons have often been associated with terrorists, but the biologist Paul Ewald noted that natural selection among pathogens is not suited to the terrorists' aim of sudden devastation.

Among the biggest real threats to human species is that of the nuclear war. Currently, the world has more than ten thousand nuclear weapons distributed among nine countries. They are mounted on missiles or loaded in bombers and are designed to unleash total annihilation. Following the bombing of Japan at the end of World War II, United States and the Soviet Union began their nuclear arms race, and a new form of historical pessimism was initiated. Some intellectuals have criticized science and modernity because of the seemingly growing nuclear threat. But Pinker notes that this criticism is misplaced, "given that since the dawn of the nuclear age, when mainstream scientists were sidelined from nuclear policy, it's been physical scientists who have waged a vociferous campaign to remind the world of the danger of nuclear war and to urge nations to disarm." However, nuclear weaponry will not be abolished in the near future. Still, each step at disarming them is a step towards our safety.

In Chapter 19 of his book, Steven Pinker discussed some of the most popular existential threats:

- Apocalypse is a plausible scenario, but many theories regarding it are unfounded.

- Real existential problems should not be observed as apocalypses, but problems that can be overcome.

- Each destroyed civilization could have used science to avert their catastrophes.

- Nuclear war is the biggest threat to human species.

- The world has more than ten thousand nuclear weapons distributed among nine countries.

- Nuclear threat will not end soon, but every step forward in disarming nuclear weapons is the reason for optimism.

Chapter 20

THE FUTURE OF PROGRESS

Previous chapters have shown us that modernity has been achieving progress in numerous aspects. Two centuries ago, the world was about 100 times poorer than today. The proportion of poor people across countries and nations has fallen from nearly 90 percent to no more than ten percent. Great famine, which has always been a part of the human history, is almost extinguished. Most children in developing countries today have smartphones, air-conditioning, and other luxuries which were once only in the possession of the rich. Racial minorities and the elderly do not face such levels of poverty as the did before. War between countries has become obsolete, and civil wars is active in only one-sixth of the global surface.

Life has become safer in almost every way. During the 20th century, the US citizens became 90 percent less likely to die in a car accident, 99 percent less likely to die in a plane accident, and 95 percent less likely to be killed at their workplace. Life is already much safer in developed countries and is bound to get safer in developing countries as they get rich. People are not only becoming safer and richer but also freer. Two-thirds of the world's countries are democratic nowadays, whereas only a handful of countries had democracy two centuries ago. Half of the world's countries used to have laws that discriminated racial minorities. Today, they have more policies to support them than the ones that discriminate them. At the beginning of the 20th century, women had a right to vote in only one country. Today, they have a right to vote in every country except one. Laws towards women, minorities, and gay are becoming more tolerant. Catastrophic nuclear wars, despite all prediction, have never happened. All in all, countries have become happier, freer, wealthier, better educated, and healthier.

Enlightenment's idea of progress has been successful. For two and a half centuries, knowledge has enabled humans to flourish. The treasury of knowledge has been sustained and increased by scholars. At the same time, however, there have been some serious problems. Each year, almost a million children die of pneumonia, more than two billion people are oppressed in autocratic countries, and almost one-fifth of people lack basic education, and every year five million people lose their lives in accidents.

Both positive and negative sides of history show us that progress is not utopia. There is always room for improvement, and indeed, this is an imperative for humanity's strive for progress. But progress will not be achieved unless we continue to foster ideals of the Enlightenment.

In Chapter 20 of his book, Steven Pinker outlined both negative and positive sides of the progress. He maintains that it is humanity's imperative to strive for the progress:

- Modernity is the proof that humanity has achieved progress by following ideals of the Enlightenment.

- There have been numerous improvements in every sector of human lives.

- There are still serious problems with conflicts, health, and death toll that necessitate solution.

- Negative side of modernity reveals that the idea of progress is not utopia.

- The only way to ensure an ongoing progress of humanity is to foster ideals of the Enlightenment and deal with problems.

Part III
Reason, Science, and Humanism

Chapter 21

REASON

W e've mentioned in the initial chapters that soon after the 18ᵗʰ century Enlightenment reached its maturity, a movement that opposed its main claims sprouted. That movement is today known as the counter-Enlightenment. Its main proponents, such as Johann Herder, favored emotions over reason and thought that scientific thinking is detrimental to human beings. Herder famously proclaimed that he is "not here to think, but to be, feel, live!" A slew of romantics soon followed this line of thought.

But to oppose reason itself is contradictory because one has to use rational arguments to do it. It would mean to *rationalize* for reasons of irrationality. Sounds like a paradox, doesn't it? One should bear in mind that not a single Enlightenment philosopher or thinker of any kind claimed that human beings were consistently rational. Not even Kant, the paragon of rationality, who wrote that "from the crooked timber of humanity no truly straight thing can be made." Most famous thinkers of the Enlightenment, such as Hume, Spinoza, and Smith argued that we *should* be rational by rejecting dogmas and fallacies that cannot be proved with rational arguments. To be rational is to *question* the dogmas of authority and challenge their validity, as Kant did in his *Critique of Pure Reason*. Certainly, human beings are prone to fallacies, superstitions, and illusions. Our cognitive capacity has evolved in a world without science and scholarship. Moreover, it is consistently pressured to process all kinds of information. The greatest challenge for modern humans is to create such informational environment in which rationality prevails over all that which leads them into folly.

But we have to ask ourselves, how is it that the modern age of scientific revolutions and breakthroughs has also brought masses of irrational people? The standard explanation for this occurrence is ignorance. Still, a huge number of people is scientifically illiterate and liable to their cognitive biases and defenseless from all sorts of information that defiles the mind. People often believe in certain propositions (be they scientific or not) on the basis of their cultural identity, and not objective reasoning. The legal scholar Dan Kahan analyzed reason in the public sphere and ascertained that most people identify with particular subcultures and tribes which has a creed of its own view of the world. Pinker reports that "psychologists have long known that the human brain is infected with motivated reasoning (directing an argument toward a favored conclusion, rather than following it where it leads), biased evaluation (finding fault with evidence that disconfirms a favored position and giving a pass to evidence that supports it), and a My-side bias (self-explanatory)."

Effective training is required in order to cure such unscientific biases and irrational thinking. But training alone is insufficient, but it also depends on, as Pinker notes, "the rules of discourse in workplaces, social circles, and arenas of debate and decision-making." Irrational and emotional biases are always present in a political discourse. We must not let them deter us from the Enlightenment ideals, which are critical for any progress.

In Chapter 21 of his book, Steven Pinker discusses the concept of reason and its role in modern Enlightenment:

- Irrationality appeared soon after the Enlightenment reached its maturity near the end of the 18th century.

- Not a single Enlightenment thinker ever claimed that we are capable of sustained rational thinking.

- Human beings will always be prone to the effects of irrationality, fantasies, dogmas. The goal is to create an informational environment in which such forms of reasoning will be purged.

- The legal scholar Dan Kahan found that our conclusions are very often affected by our cultural identity and not (only) by objective reasoning.

- Biased and irrational thinking today is part of any political discourse. We must not let them discourage us from rational ideals.

Chapter 22

SCIENCE

S cience is the proudest achievement of the modern world. Talking about humanity's greatest achievements, most people would list the abolishment of slavery and the destruction of fascism. But those are the evils humanity has brought upon itself. Science, however, is an all-embracing merit of the modern world. It has flourished to such an extent that today we are able to explain the origin of most things, talk about the history of the universe, and assess the structure of our life and cognitive capacities. Of course, there are still so many things that we don't know (and possibly will never know), but the amount of knowledge that science helped us accumulate is astonishing. For instance, the physicist Sean Carroll has argued that the laws of physics that underlie our everyday life are known *in toto*. Carroll concludes such achievement is certainly one of humanity's greatest.

Science continues to astound and produce things of exquisite beauty. It has enabled us to deepen our understanding of the world, answer what was formerly unanswerable. Science shed a new light on our life and the outside world. It granted gifts such as health, life, wealth, freedom, and knowledge. The fact that science alone allowed us to eradicate smallpox, the disease that wiped out 300 million people in the 20th century is enough reject all absurd claims that we live in an age of global decline and meaninglessness. In our age, many intellectuals are hostile towards science. Pinker notes that "in the major journals of opinion, scientific carpetbaggers are regularly accused of determinism, reductionism, essentialism, positivism, and, worst of all, a crime called scientism." The prosecution has been active with both right and left-wing intellectuals. For instance, the case for the left can be found in a review by the historian Jacks Lears: "Positivism depends on the reductionist belief that the entire universe, including all human conduct, can be explained with reference to precisely measurable, deterministic physical processes. [...] Two world wars, the systematic slaughter of innocents on an unprecedented scale, the proliferation of unimaginably destructive weapons, [...] – all these events involved, in various degrees, the application of scientific research to advanced technology."

The case for the right-wing criticism of science came from Leon Kass, George Bush's bioethics advisor: "Scientific ideas and discoveries about living nature and man, perfectly welcome and harmless in themselves, are being enlisted to do battle against our traditional religious and moral teachings, and even our self-understanding as creatures with freedom and dignity." What most critics of science fail to recognize is that science is not about claiming access to universal knowledge, or that a certain hypothesis must be true. True, many scientific hypotheses are false. But taking that to mean that science itself cannot be trusted is fallacious reasoning. Science was never simply a list of empirical facts. Scientists are constantly within an ethereal sphere of information coming from mathematics, physics, or logic. There is no such thing as a strictly "scientific method." Scientists use all methods that help them understand and describe the world.

In Chapter 22 of his book, Steven Pinker critically analyzed positive aspects and criticism of science:

- Science should be recognized as the greatest achievement of humanity.

- Science has allowed us to deepen our knowledge of the world and understand it better.

- The critics of science fail to realize that science can be right or wrong about things. If it is wrong, it doesn't mean we should reject it.

- There is not a strict "scientific method," as science uses all methods to understand the world.

- Scientists constantly use the information coming from mathematics, logic, or physics.

Chapter 23

HUMANISM

Baruch Spinoza famously declared that "those who are governed by reason desire nothing for themselves which they do not also desire for the rest of humankind." Progress is about using knowledge to enable all humankind to flourish such that all of us desire to flourish. Humanism means maximizing the flourishing of health, life, freedom, knowledge, happiness, and richness of experience. It defines what we *ought to* try to achieve with our knowledge. A movement called Humanism, which is currently active and growing, promotes a non-supernatural basis for ethics and meaning: good without God. Their *Humanist Manifesto* (2003) affirms the following:

- Knowledge of the world is derived by observation, experimentation, and rational analysis.

- Humans are an integral part of nature, the result of unguided evolutionary change.

- Ethical values are derived from human need and interest as tested by experience.

- Life's fulfillment emerges from individual participation in the service of humane ideals.

- Humans are social by nature and find meaning in relationship.

- Working to benefit society maximizes individual happiness.

Strands of humanism existed in the ancient past but sprouted forth in the Age of Reason and Enlightenment. Humanism was further bolstered by creation of the United Nations, the Universal Declaration of Humans Rights, and other global cooperation institutions that were established after World War II.

Kant's categorical imperative or Spinoza's famous dictum are the moral foundations for *impartiality*: "Do not do to others that which you would not done to yourself." However, arguments for partiality do not have developed content. Anyone could list their own arguments with regard to this dictum. The Declaration of Independence states that the rights to liberty, life, and the pursuit of happiness are "self-evident." That, however, is not always the case. However, it captures the essence of humanity: one does not have to justify life when examining the foundations of morality. The appeal for regressive ideas, such as the existence of God, is perennial. The case for reason, science, progress, and humanity always has to be made. These are the gifts of the Enlightenment that has pushed us forward in the course of history.

In the final Chapter 23 of his book, Steven Pinker discussed the concept of humanity as one of the principle Enlightenment's ideals:

- The idea of progress is about using knowledge to benefit all humankind.

- Humanism means maximizing the flourishing of health, life, freedom, knowledge, happiness, and richness of experience.

- The point of humanism is to define what we should try to achieve with our knowledge.

- The idea of humanism rose to prominence during Enlightenment and again after World War II.

- The case of reason, science, humanism, and progress always has to be made.

How open minded would you be about trying this as a path to spread your generosity?

Beloved reader, this is a note from Antonio, founder of Better.me. First of all, I would like you to thank you for your time to read this summary. I wish that it helped you.

I bet that if you are a bit like me, you enjoy reading and seek for knowledge as a daily basis, not as a burden or a must do, but as an enjoyable path of being a constant learner.

Based on that, I'd like to ask you how open-minded you are about providing us a review on Amazon?

It's a 30-second process and all you have to do is:

1) Log in into your Amazon account

2) Access this link - https://www.amazon.com/review/create-review?asin=B06Y1G6Z3Z#

3) Write in a few words your thoughts on the book and choose a rating. Does not have to be big, just a sentence will help. The title is optional so do it if you want it too.

If you leave it a review, you will be contributing to the publishing of more summaries

Always keep learning!

Thanks in advance,

Kind regards

Antonio Monteiro from Better.me

Beyond Biocentrism:
Rethinking Time, Space,
Consciousness, & the
Illusion of Death
By Dr. Robert Lanza

Made in the USA
San Bernardino, CA
06 May 2018